Fondue Favorites Cookbook: 60 Super #Delish Fondue Recipes

RHONDA BELLE

DEDICATION

To Foodies Everywhere...Enjoy & Be Well!

Table of Contents

Fondue How-To: 8

Fondue Dippers: 8

    AGED CHEDDAR BREW FONDUE...9

    ALMIGHTY ALMOND FONDUE 9

    BACON CHEESE FONDUE (alcohol) 10

    BLOOMING ONION FONDUE..10

    BLUE FONDUE (alcohol)...11

    BOUQUET O' ROSES FONDUE (alcohol) 11

    BUTTERSCOTCH FONDUE..11

    CHEDDAR ZIPPER FONDUE 12

    CHEESE & CIDER FONDUE 12

    CHIPOTLE BACON FONDUE (alcohol)..12

    CHOCO-CHIP MARSHMALLOW FONDUE 13

    CINNAMON CHOCOLATE FONDUE (alcohol) 13

    CLASSIC CHEESE FONDUE 13

    CLASSIC SWISS CHEESE FONDUE (alcohol) 14

    COCO-CROCK FONDUE 14

    COCONUT FONDUE 14

    CRAZY FOR CRANBERRIES FONDUE 15

    CREAMY CARAMEL FONDUE (alcohol optional)..15

    CREAMY MUSHROOM FONDUE..15

    CURRY CHILI FONDUE 16

    EVERYDAY CHEDDAR FONDUE 16

    EXTRA CHEESEY FONDUE 17

    FESTIVE HOLIDAY FONDUE 17

    FETA & RICOTTA CHEESE FONDUE...17

    FIG & NUT FONDUE...18

    FONDUE FIX (alcohol)..18

    FRUIT & CAKE FONDUE 19

    GARLIC GOODNESS FONDUE (alcohol)..19

    HAZELNUT HEAVEN FONDUE 19

    HEATWAVE CHILI FONDUE 20

    KISS ME I'M IRISH FONDUE (alcohol) 20

    LEMON FONDUE..20

MERRY MOCHA FONDUE 21

MEXICAN CHEESE FONDUE..21

PEANUT BUTTER LOVER FONDUE 21

PERFECT PESTO FONDUE (alcohol) 22

PRALINE FONDUE..22

PRETTY PLUM FONDUE (alcohol) 22

QUICKIE CROCKPOT FONDUE 23

RAW VEGAN SPECIAL FONDUE 23

SAVORY BROTH FONDUE..23

SHRIMP & CHEESE FONDUE..24

SIMPLE MILK CHOCOLATE FONDUE (alcohol optional).........................24

SKINNY CHOCOLATE FONDUE 24

SPECTACULAR SPINACH FONDUE (large batch) 25

SPICY CRAB FONDUE (alcohol) 25

STRAWBERRY FIELDS FONDUE 25

SUBLIME SWEETCORN FONDUE...26

TANGERINE DREAM FONDUE 26

TERRIFIC TERIYAKI FONDUE (alcohol)...26

TOMATO GARDEN FONDUE (alcohol) 27

TOTALLY TOFFEE FONDUE 27

VEGETARIAN DELIGHT FONDUE..28

VEGGIE VICTORY FONDUE 28

VELVET ROPE FONDUE..29

VERY BERRY FONDUE..29

VERY VEGAN POTATO FONDUE (alcohol)...29

WHITE CREAM FONDUE (alcohol) 30

WHITE WINE SWIRL FONDUE (alcohol) 30

WORLD TRAVELER CHEESE FONDUE (alcohol)..30

Bonus 31

TURTLE FLAMBE FONDUE (alcohol) 31

DIABETIC CHOCOLATE FONDUE 31

ACKNOWLEDGEMENTS

To the love of my life, Johnny.
You are Mommy's greatest inspiration.

To my Mom & Dad (Sunset February 2016)
Love you both...always!

Fondue How-To:

Fondue is both delicious and fun! When serving cheese or chocolate fondue, fondue forks should be used to spear dippers. Partakers should pause to allow drips to flow back into the pot and then transfer their yummy morsels to a plate. Fondue is then eaten with a table fork. If you're going more casual or intimate, eating direct from the fondue fork is fine. *Note that meat fondue gets extremely hot. If eating from the skewer, exercise caution.*

Many of the cheeses used in fondue are artisanal varieties found in the specialty section of your local supermarket. Also, alcohol is common in many recipes and give fondue a special flavor. In most cases, it can be considered optional. If you do not have a fondue pot, a small slow cooker also works well.

Fondue Dippers:

Breads, cookies, and fresh fruits and veggies make excellent fondue dippers. Try these great accompaniments with your next fondue experience:
Breadsticks
Brownie bites
Chopped celery
Chunks of gourmet and/or loafy baked breads
Dried cranberries or fruit pieces
Fresh strawberries
Fruit pieces (pear, pineapple, apple, banana, oranges, and strawberries)
Graham crackers
Juicy grape or cherry tomatoes
Marshmallows
Melon balls
Raw or pickled veggies such as onions, broccoli or carrots
Pitted green or black olives
Portobello or button mushrooms
Pound-cake cubes
Rice Krispie treats
Roasted or raw pepper, zucchini or cucumber strips
Rosemary new potatoes
Shortbread cookies
Small gherkins
Soft pretzels
Vanilla wafers

Also consider a range of meat options. Excellent choices to cube or chunk include:

Fried Andouille or Lil' Smokies Sausages
Chicken Breast
Chicken, Veggie or Seafood Ravioli Pot Stickers
Filet Mignon
Lobster
Meatballs
Peeled Shrimp
Pork Tenderloin
Sashimi Tuna
Scallops

Have a culinary adventure by mixing and matching dippers in the following fabulous fondue recipes. Enjoy!

AGED CHEDDAR BREW FONDUE

1 lb. good aged cheddar, grated
1 teaspoon finely minced garlic
1 teaspoon powdered mustard
1 teaspoon Worcestershire sauce
2 ½ tablespoons all-purpose flour
2 teaspoons olive oil
6 tablespoons frozen apple juice concentrate, thawed
8 oz. Guinness Extra Stout beer

Toast bread: If your bread is day-old, skip this step. Otherwise cut the bread into 1" squares. Turn oven to 250F. Toast bread pieces for 15 minutes. Remove and cool.

Make fondue: Toss grated cheese with the flour. In your fondue pot over low heat, add 2 teaspoons of olive oil and garlic. Fry until garlic is fragrant, about 30 seconds. Turn heat to medium-high. Add Guinness, apple juice concentrate, Worcestershire sauce and mustard. Bring to boil. Add cheese a little at a time, stirring constantly until fondue is smooth and melted. Thin with more Guinness, if needed throughout the meal. Season with salt and pepper.

ALMIGHTY ALMOND FONDUE

¼ teaspoon salt
½ cup sugar
1 ¼ teaspoons almond extract
1 tablespoon butter
2 cups half-and-half cream
2 egg yolks, beaten
2 tablespoons cornstarch

In a large heavy saucepan, combine the sugar, cornstarch and salt. Stir in cream until smooth. Cook and stir over medium-high heat until thickened and bubbly. Reduce heat; cook and stir 2 minutes longer. Remove from the heat. Stir a small amount of hot mixture into egg yolks; return all to the pan, stirring constantly. Bring to a gentle boil; cook and stir 2 minutes longer. Remove from the heat; stir in butter and extract. Keep warm. Serve with brownies, cake, waffles and/or cookies.

BACON CHEESE FONDUE (alcohol)
1 cup light beer
1 tablespoon bourbon
2 ¾ cups (11 ounces) shredded cheddar cheese
2 tablespoons chopped cooked bacon
2 teaspoons dry mustard
2 teaspoons freshly ground pepper
2 teaspoons Worcestershire sauce
3 tablespoons all-purpose flour
4 teaspoons chopped scallions
4 teaspoons prepared horseradish

Toss the cheese with the flour in a bowl. Place a metal bowl over a saucepan, or double boiler, filled with two inches of water. Bring the water to a boil over high heat. Reduce the heat to medium and pour the beer into the bowl. Stir in the horseradish, mustard and Worcestershire sauce using a fork. Cook for 30 seconds, stirring constantly. Add half the cheese and cook until the cheese is melted, stirring constantly. Add the remaining cheese a small amount at a time, stirring constantly in a circular motion after each addition until the cheese is melted. Pour in the bourbon slowly around the edge of the bowl. Pull the cheese mixture away from the edge of the bowl and cook for about 30 seconds or until the alcohol cooks off. Stir the bourbon into the cheese Fold in the bacon and pepper. Pour into a warm fondue pot and keep warm over low heat. Garnish with scallions and use dippers of your choice.

BLOOMING ONION FONDUE
¾ cup unsalted butter
1 teaspoon chicken stock base
12 ounces pepper jack cheese
5 large onions, thinly sliced
8 cups beef broth
French or sourdough bread sliced 1" thick.
White pepper

Melt butter in large kettle. Add onions and sauté until transparent. *Do not brown.* Add beef broth and chicken stock base. Cover and simmer 2 - 3 hours. Remove from heat and refrigerate overnight or at least for several hours.

Discard any chilled surface fat. Reheat and season to taste with white pepper. Slice cheese into 12 slices. Lightly toast 12 bread slices and top each with 1 slice pepper jack cheese. Pour soup into individual ovenproof serving bowls and top with slice of bread and cheese. *If you wish, run bowls under broiler just until cheese bubbles and is soft, but not brown.*

BLUE FONDUE (alcohol)

1 cup dry white wine
1 tablespoon cornstarch
2 cups (8 ounces) crumbled blue cheese
2/3 cup 1% low-fat milk
One 8-ounce block fat-free cream cheese, softened

Combine the blue cheese and the cornstarch in a large saucepan. Stir in wine, milk, and cream cheese. Bring to a boil over medium heat; cook for 1 minute, stirring constantly. Reduce heat to medium-low; cook 8 minutes or until mixture is smooth, stirring frequently. Pour into a fondue pot with its own heat source. Use dippers of your choice.

BOUQUET O' ROSES FONDUE (alcohol)

1 clove garlic, halved
2 teaspoon Kirsch
3 teaspoons corn flour
4 ounces grated Gruyere cheese
8 ounces grated red-veined cheddar cheese
8 ounces rose wine

Rub the inside of the fondue pot with the cut side of the garlic. Add the wine and heat until bubbling, then gradually stir in the cheeses until melted, stirring frequently. In a small bowl, blend the corn flour smoothly with the Kirsch and stir into the cheese mixture. Cook for a couple of minutes until smooth and thickened, stirring frequently. Serve with cubes of French bread.

BUTTERSCOTCH FONDUE

¾ cup whole milk
1 cup smooth peanut butter
2 tablespoons of boiling water
Two 11 ounce bags butterscotch morsels

In a medium saucepan, warm the milk over medium heat. Add the butterscotch chips and cook, stirring, until smooth, about 10 minutes; remove from heat. Whisk in the peanut butter until smooth. Stir in the boiling water. Serve warm with 1 inch pieces of bacon and/or apples, pretzel rods, and marshmallows.

CHEDDAR ZIPPER FONDUE

1 cup beer light beer
1 tablespoon chopped scallions
2 - 3 cups (11 oz.) shredded Cheddar cheese
2 tablespoons chopped cooked bacon
2 teaspoons freshly ground pepper
2 teaspoons Worcestershire sauce
3 tablespoons all-purpose flour
4 teaspoons dry mustard
4 teaspoons prepared horseradish

Toss the cheese with the flour in a bowl. Place a metal bowl over a saucepan filled with 2 inches of water. You may also use a conventional double boiler. Bring the water to a boil over high heat. Reduce the heat to medium and pour the beer into the bowl. Press the liquid from the horseradish. Stir the horseradish, Worcestershire sauce and mustard into beer using a fork. Cook for 30 seconds, stirring constantly.
Add half the cheese and cook until the cheese is melted, stirring constantly. Add the remaining cheese a small amount at a time, stirring constantly in a circular motion after each addition until the cheese is melted. Fold in the bacon and pepper. Pour into a warm fondue pot and keep warm over low heat. Garnish with the scallions. Serves four to six.

CHEESE & CIDER FONDUE

¾ cup apple cider or apple juice
1 cup (4 ounces) shredded Swiss cheese
1 tablespoon cornstarch
1/8 teaspoon pepper
2 cups (8 ounces) shredded cheddar cheese

In a large saucepan, bring cider to a boil. Reduce heat to medium-low. Toss the cheeses with cornstarch and pepper; stir into cider. Cook and stir for 3-4 minutes or until cheese is melted.   Transfer to a small fondue pot with its own heat source. Use cubed French bread as a dipper!

CHIPOTLE BACON FONDUE (alcohol)

1 cup white wine
1 tablespoon chopped scallions
1 teaspoon freshly ground pepper
2 tablespoons all-purpose flour
2 tablespoons chopped cooked bacon
2 teaspoons finely chopped garlic
3 ½ cups (14 ounces) shredded Swiss cheese
4 teaspoons finely chopped chipotle chili

Toss the cheese with the flour in a bowl. Place a metal bowl over a saucepan, or double boiler, filled with two inches of water. Bring the water to a boil over high heat. Reduce the heat to medium and pour the wine into the bowl. Stir in the garlic using a fork. Cook for 30 seconds, stirring constantly. Add half the cheese and cook until melted, stirring constantly. Add the remaining cheese a small amount at a time, stirring constantly in a circular motion after each addition until the cheese is melted. Fold in the chili, bacon and pepper. Pour into a warm fondue pot and keep warm over low heat. Use dippers of choice.

CHOCO-CHIP MARSHMALLOW FONDUE
½ cup milk
1 can (14 ounces) sweetened condensed milk
1 jar (7 ounces) marshmallow creme
1 teaspoon vanilla extract
2 cups (12 ounces) semi-sweet chocolate chips
In a microwave or heavy saucepan, heat the first five ingredients until just melted; whisk until smooth. Transfer to a fondue pot with its own heat source. Serve with pineapple or banana chunks, apple slices, marshmallows, cubed cake chunks.

CINNAMON CHOCOLATE FONDUE (alcohol)
¼ cup flour
¼ cup Kahlua
¼ cup margarine
½ teaspoon cinnamon
2 cups light corn syrup
8 ounces bittersweet chocolate
Melt margarine and chocolate. Whisk in flour until blended; cook 1 minute, stirring. Remove from heat, blend in cinnamon. Pour into fondue dish with its own heat source. Suggested dippers are bananas, strawberries, oranges, and pound food chunks.

CLASSIC CHEESE FONDUE
1 clove garlic, halved
1 cup apple juice
1 teaspoon cornstarch
3 teaspoons lemon juice
9 ounces Emmenthaler cheese
9 ounces Gruyere Cheese
Dashes of paprika and freshly ground nutmeg
Grate cheeses. Rub fondue pot with garlic. Add the apple juice and heat slowly. Once bubbly, stir in cheese by the handful. While the cheese is melting, mix

cornstarch and lemon juice until smooth. Stir into cheese mixture until thick. Season with paprika and nutmeg. Transfer to fondue pot to serve with your favorite dipper.

CLASSIC SWISS CHEESE FONDUE (alcohol)
1 garlic clove, cut in half
1 lb. Emmenthaler or Gruyere cheese, or a 50-50 mix, finely cut (not grated)
2 cup dry white wine, Neuchatel, Rhine or Chablis
2 loaves crusty French or Italian bread
3 tablespoon cornstarch
3 tablespoon Kirsh or brandy
Pinch of nutmeg
Salt & black pepper to taste
Rub fondue pot walls with cut garlic. Pour in wine and bring to a simmer over low heat. *Do not boil.* Gradually stir in cheese bits, when melted, stir in corn starch that has been dissolved in chosen alcohol. Add salt, pepper and nutmeg, stir and bring to a simmer. Keep cheese bubbling lightly over low heat to prevent thickening. Serve with bread cubes, a tossed side salad or a selection of fruits for dessert.

COCO-CROCK FONDUE
½ cup whipping cream
1 ½ cup marshmallows, miniature
1 ½ teaspoons butter or margarine
3 tablespoons milk
8 pack of chocolate candy bars with almonds of your choice (1 ounce size)
Coat fondue or crockpot walls with butter. Place candy bars, milk, and marshmallows inside and cover and cook, stirring every 30 minutes until melted and smooth. Gradually add whipping cream. Be sure your chosen fondue dish has its own heat source to keep warm. Serve with bite size pieces of angel food cake, yellow cake, bananas, strawberries, grapes, and mandarin oranges.

COCONUT FONDUE
2 ounces creamed coconut, chopped
2 ounces sugar
3 ounces dried coconut
4 teaspoons corn flour
5 ounces single cream
Put the dried coconut in a saucepan with 16 ounces of water, the creamed coconut and sugar. Bring to the boil and simmer for 10 minutes. Strain the mixture into a bowl, pressing mixture thoroughly to extract all the liquid. In a

fondue pot, blend the corn flour smoothly with the cream, then add the coconut liquid, and cook over a gentle heat until thickened, stirring all the time. Use dippers of your choice.

CRAZY FOR CRANBERRIES FONDUE
1 cup hard cider
1 teaspoon freshly ground pepper
2 - 3 cups (11 oz.) shredded Cheddar cheese
2 tablespoons chopped sweetened dried cranberries
2 teaspoons crushed walnuts
2 teaspoons dry mustard
2 teaspoons finely chopped shallots
3 tablespoons all-purpose flour
Toss the cheese with the flour in a bowl. Place a metal bowl over a saucepan, or double boiler, filled with two inches of water. Bring the water to a boil over high heat. Reduce the heat to medium and pour the hard cider into the bowl. Stir in the shallots, mustard and cranberries using a fork. Cook for 30 seconds stirring constantly. Add half of the cheese, and stir constantly until melted. Add the remaining cheese a small amount at a time stirring constantly. Stir in the pepper. Pour into a warm fondue pot and keep warm over low heat. Garnish with walnuts and use dippers of your choice.

CREAMY CARAMEL FONDUE (alcohol optional)
1 teaspoon vanilla extract
3 tablespoons brandy (optional)
6 ounces (about 24) caramels
One 13-ounce can of evaporated milk
Heat the milk and caramels in a heavy saucepan over a low heat, stirring occasionally, until all the caramels are melted. Increase the heat a little, and simmer for 3 or 4 minutes until slightly thickened. Remove from heat and stir in brandy and vanilla extract. Perfect for apple and banana dippers.

CREAMY MUSHROOM FONDUE
¼ cup butter (about 2 ounces)
1 lb. mushrooms, finely chopped
2 cloves garlic, crushed
2/3 cup chicken stock
2/3 cup double (thick) cream
3 teaspoons corn flour
Salt and black pepper to taste
Pinch of cayenne pepper

Melt butter in a saucepan, add mushrooms and garlic and cook gently for 10 minutes. Add stock and simmer for 10 minutes. Cool slightly and puree in a blender or food processor. Put a little cream into the fondue pot, blend in corn flour smoothly. Next, add remaining cream and mushroom puree. Heat to simmer and cook over a gentle heat until thickened, stirring frequently. Season to taste, including the cayenne. Try this one with cubes of cheese and garlic sausage.

CURRY CHILI FONDUE
½ cup fresh cream
½ cup milk
¼ teaspoon sea salt
¾ teaspoon red chili flakes
½ teaspoon crushed garlic paste
½ teaspoon curry powder
½ teaspoon roasted white cumin seeds
1/3 teaspoon grated mozzarella
Heat milk & cheese in a saucepan and keep stirring till cheese melts. Transfer mixture to a fondue bowl. Stir in the remaining ingredients & mix well. Recommended dippers include sliced cucumbers, carrots and breadsticks.

EVERYDAY CHEDDAR FONDUE
¼ cup all-purpose flour
¼ cup butter or margarine
¼ teaspoon ground mustard
¼ teaspoon pepper
¼ teaspoon Worcestershire sauce
½ teaspoon salt, optional
1 ½ cups milk
2 cups (8 ounces) shredded cheddar cheese
In a saucepan, melt butter; stir in flour, salt if desired, pepper, mustard, and Worcestershire sauce until smooth. Gradually add milk. Bring to a boil; cook and stir until thickened. Reduce heat. Add the cheese; cook and stir until melted and smooth. Transfer to fondue pot with its own heat source. Suggested dippers include bread cubes, ham cubes, sausage, and/or broccoli florets.

EXTRA CHEESEY FONDUE
½ cup grated cheese blend (Cheddar, Monterey Jack and Swiss)
1 cup milk
2 tablespoons flour
2 tablespoons margarine
Dried minced onions
Salt and black pepper to taste
Melt butter in saucepan. Remove from heat. Add flour. Whisk till smooth. Add milk in small amounts, whisking until smooth after each addition. Place back on medium heat. Stir constantly to thicken. Add salt, pepper and onions to taste. Lastly, add cheese. Bread, meatballs or steamed veggies make great dippers.

FESTIVE HOLIDAY FONDUE
¼ teaspoon garlic powder
½ lb. ground beef
1 ½ teaspoons fennel seeds
1 ½ teaspoons leaf oregano
1 cup (4 ounces) mozzarella cheese
1 medium onion, chopped
2 ½ cups (10 ounces) shredded cheddar cheese
2 cans (10 ½ ounces) pizza sauce
In a sauce pan over medium heat, brown onion and ground beef. Drain. Add pizza sauce and seasonings; stir until heated. Add cheese by handfuls. Stir until smooth. Pour into fondue pot with its own heat source to keep mix warm. Recommended dippers include Italian or French bread cubes.

FETA & RICOTTA CHEESE FONDUE
1 cup ricotta cheese
1/8 teaspoon pepper
3 tablespoons butter or margarine
4 ounces feta cheese cubes (about ½ inch each)
Juice of 1 lemon
1 tablespoon parsley, minced (optional)
Melt the butter in a heavy 8-inch skillet or a 1 quart saucepan over low-heat. Add the feta and ricotta cheese, and pepper. Cook, stirring constantly, and mashing the cheeses slightly, until they soften and begin to bubble - about 5 minutes. Stir in lemon juice, and garnish with the parsley if desired. Pour into fondue pot with its own heat source to keep mix warm. Use dippers of your choice.

FIG & NUT FONDUE

¼ cup toasted pecans, ground
¼ teaspoon fresh ground black pepper
½ cup dry white wine
½ cup fig preserves
½ lb. Emmenthaler cheese, grated (2 cups)
½ lb. Gruyere cheese, grated (2 cups)
1 tablespoon fresh lemon juice
2 tablespoons cornstarch
Grated fresh nutmeg (a little sprinkling)

In a medium saucepan over medium heat, combine the wine, fig preserves, pecans, and lemon juice.

Cook, stirring often, until the preserves are melted. In a bowl, combine the cheeses, cornstarch, pepper, and nutmeg. Stir the cheese mixture into the preserves one small handful at a time, making sure that each handful is completely melted before adding the next. The fondue can bubble a bit, but don't let it boil.

Transfer the cheese mixture to a warm fondue pot and keep warm over a burner. Stir occasionally. Serve right away with cubes of pumpernickel and sourdough bread for dipping.

FONDUE FIX (alcohol)

3 tbsp. all-purpose flour
2 tsp. chopped shallots
1 tsp. freshly ground pepper
2 tbsp. chopped scallions
1 and 1/2 cups (6 oz.) shredded Swiss cheese
1 and 1/2 cups (6 oz.) shredded fontina cheese
1/4 cup dry sherry
1/4 cup crumbled Blue cheese
3/4 cup white wine

Toss the cheeses with the flour in a bowl. Place a metal bowl over a saucepan, or double boiler, filled with two inches of water. Bring the water to a boil over high heat. Reduce the heat to medium and pour the wine and sherry into the bowl. Stir in the shallots using a fork. Cook for 30 seconds stirring constantly. Add half of the cheese blend, and stir constantly until melted. Add the remaining cheese blend a small amount at a time stirring constantly. Fold in the pepper and blue cheese. Pour into a warm fondue pot and keep warm over low heat. Garnish with scallions and use dippers of your choice.

FRUIT & CAKE FONDUE

¼ cup (plus 2 teaspoons) orange liqueur
½ cup butter
1 ½ cups sugar
1 cup Half-&-Half creamer
1/8 teaspoon salt
6 ounces unsweetened chocolate

In saucepan, melt butter and chocolate over low heat. Add sugar, Half-and-Half and salt. Bring to a boil, cook over med. heat at a slow rolling boil, stirring constantly for 5 minutes until thickened. Cover and refrigerate until needed. When ready, heat sauce in microwave up to 230 seconds. Add liqueur and stir to combine thoroughly. Pour into fondue pot with its own heat source to keep mix warm. Serve immediately with fruit and cake.

GARLIC GOODNESS FONDUE (alcohol)

½ cup extra dry champagne
2 cans water
2 cans chicken broth (10 ¾ ounces each)
3 tablespoons butter
4 slices French bread
4 slices Gruyere cheese
40 cloves fresh garlic, minced
Cayenne pepper to taste
Minced chives

Sauté garlic in butter for 10 minutes, stirring often. *Careful not to brown.* Add broth, water, champagne and simmer 5 minutes. Toast bread. Ladle soup into bowls. Float bread on top of soup, sprinkle with cheese and bake at 475 degrees, uncovered, for 15 minutes. Sprinkle with cayenne and chives. Serve with your choice of meat or veggie dippers.

HAZELNUT HEAVEN FONDUE

½ ounce unsweetened chocolate, chopped
½ teaspoon vanilla extract
1 can (14 ounces) fat-free sweetened condensed milk
2 tablespoons unsweetened cocoa powder
3 tablespoons chocolate-hazelnut spread
Pinch of salt

In a small nonstick saucepan, combine the chocolate and about half of the condensed milk. Heat over medium heat for 3 minutes, stirring until the chocolate is melted. Remove from the heat and stir in the remaining milk. Sift the cocoa and salt on top. Stir until blended. Return to the heat and cook, stirring, for 3 minutes longer, or until the fondue just begins to simmer.

Remove from the heat. Stir in the chocolate-hazelnut spread and vanilla until smooth. Serve warm with assorted fruit pieces and cake cubes.

HEATWAVE CHILI FONDUE
¼ teaspoon hot pepper flakes
½ cup chicken broth
½ cup water
1 tablespoon low-sodium soy sauce
1 teaspoon granulated sugar
2 tablespoons lemon or lime juice
Combine all ingredients. Pour into fondue pot with its own heat source to keep mix warm and simmer meat of your choice.

KISS ME I'M IRISH FONDUE (alcohol)
1 cup Guinness Extra Stout beer
1 teaspoon Worcestershire sauce
2 - 3 cups (11 oz.) shredded Cheddar cheese
2 tablespoons chives, chopped
2 teaspoons Tabasco sauce
3 tablespoons all-purpose flour
4 teaspoons dry mustard powder
Toss cheese with flour to thicken. Turn heat source to high, place pot with 1" water on burner. Place liner into pot. When steam is visible, reduce heat to medium. Add beer to liner. While stirring with a fork; add Worcestershire sauce, mustard powder, and Tabasco. Stir for approximately 30 seconds. Add ½ of cheese and stir until mix becomes liquid. Then add small pinches of cheese, stirring using a circular whipping motion until smooth. Remove fork and garnish with chopped chives. Veggies go great with this one.

LEMON FONDUE
½ cup butter or margarine
½ cup cornstarch
½ cup lemon juice
1 cup sugar
2 tablespoons grated lemon peel
4 cups water
In a heavy saucepan, combine sugar, cornstarch and salt. Stir in water until smooth. Bring to a boil over medium heat; cook and stir for 1-2 minutes or until thickened. Remove from the heat; stir in butter, lemon juice and peel until butter is melted. Transfer to a fondue pot and keep warm. Serve with strawberries, gingerbread, or other light pastries.

MERRY MOCHA FONDUE

½ cup sifted powdered sugar
1 teaspoon instant coffee crystals
2 tablespoons coffee liqueur
2/3 cup light cream or milk
4 ounces semisweet chocolate, chopped
One 4-ounce package sweet baking chocolate, broken up
In a heavy saucepan combine chocolates, cream, sugar, and coffee crystals. Heat and stir over low heat until melted and smooth. Remove from heat; stir in liqueur. Pour into a fondue pot; keep warm over low heat. Serve with fruit or cookies.

MEXICAN CHEESE FONDUE

¼ onion
1 pound Manchego or Monterey Jack cheese
2 cloves garlic
2 large tomatoes
2 teaspoons oil
3 chopped serrano or jalapeno peppers (or a small can of Rotel mixed peppers)
Salt to taste
Cook tomatoes with the peppers and very little water. Then blend in peppers, garlic and onion. Sauté the sauce with oil, and salt. Let it cook for a few minutes. Add the cheese in small pieces. Pour into fondue pot with its own heat source to keep mix warm.   For a fun dipping option, try flour tortilla pieces.

PEANUT BUTTER LOVER FONDUE

½ cup peanut butter
12 ounces semisweet chocolate chips
Lemon juice
Melt chocolate and stir in peanut butter until melted smooth. Use marshmallows, fruit or angel food cubes to dip!

PERFECT PESTO FONDUE (alcohol)

½ cup grated Pecorino Romano cheese
1 ½ cups grated Swiss cheese
1 ½ cups grated imported Fontina cheese
1 clove garlic, halved
1 cup Italian dry white wine
1/2 cup of your favorite basic pesto
2 to 3 tablespoons unbleached all-purpose flower

Rub walls of fondue pot with the garlic. Pour in the wine and heat over medium-low heat until hot. Add cheeses a hand full at a time, to the wine, stirring constantly and waiting until each addition melts before adding the next. Check the consistency and adjust as needed. Just before serving, swirl the pesto over the top of the fondue. Serve with 1" pieces of fried Italian sausage, cubes of French bread, pineapples, and/or cherry tomatoes.

PRALINE FONDUE

4 ounces caster sugar
4 ounces blanched almonds
8 ounces white chocolate
5 ounces double cream
A few drops of vanilla extract

To make the praline: Oil a baking sheet. Put the sugar and almonds into a small saucepan. Place over a low heat and leave until the sugar turns into a golden liquid. Pour at once onto the oiled baking sheet, then leave to cool and harden for 15 minutes. Coarsely break up the praline, the put into a food processor and process until finely ground. For fondue: Put chocolate and cream into a fondue pot and heat gently until the chocolate melts, stirring all the time. Stir in the praline and flavor with a few drops of vanilla extract. Goes great with cubes of cake and fresh fruit of your choice.

PRETTY PLUM FONDUE (alcohol)

½ cup sugar
½ teaspoon ground cinnamon
1 ½ lbs. red or yellow plums
2 tablespoons ginger wine
4 teaspoons corn flour

Cut plums in half and discard pits. Put the plums into a saucepan with sugar and cinnamon and 10 ounces of water. Cover and simmer for 15 minutes. In a small bowl, blend corn flour smoothly with wine and stir into plum puree. Heat gently, stirring until thickened. Pour into fondue pot with its own heat source to keep mix warm. Serve with cubes of lemon sponge cake and slices of fruit.

QUICKIE CROCKPOT FONDUE

½ teaspoon nutmeg
1 teaspoon ground white pepper
1.5 lbs. processed Swiss cheese, shredded or finely diced
1/8 teaspoon cayenne pepper
3 cloves garlic, peeled and crushed
3 cups dry white wine (such as Chardonnay)

Plug in a small slow cooker and set it to the "warm" setting. Place the white wine, crushed garlic cloves, cayenne pepper, white pepper, and nutmeg in a saucepan over medium heat. After five minutes, turn the heat down to low and let it simmer for 10 minutes. Meanwhile, place the processed Swiss cheese into the slow cooker and cover with the lid. After the wine has reduced for 10 minutes, pour it directly over the cheese in the crockpot (you may want to remove the crock from the heating element before doing this, so you don't spill liquid over the electric parts). Use a whisk to combine the cheese with the wine mixture. It will seem like it is not working at first, but it will soon come together. If after a few minutes there are still large chunks, turn the heat up to high and let it cook for 5-10 minutes. Whisk until smooth. Serve with pretzels, sourdough or rye bread, or sausage.

RAW VEGAN SPECIAL FONDUE

¼ cup raw cacao powder
¼ cup agave nectar
1 teaspoon vanilla extract
2 tablespoons coconut oil liquid
2-3 cups organic fruit to dip

Pour heated coconut oil into a bowl and add the other three ingredients. Beat together with wire whisk and quickly begin to dip chosen fruit pieces before the chocolate starts to thicken. You can also lay out your covered pieces on wax paper for the refrigerator or freezer. Ready to enjoy within minutes!

SAVORY BROTH FONDUE

¼ cup chopped fresh cilantro
¼ cup orange juice, fresh squeezed
1 teaspoon minced garlic
2 teaspoons cracked black pepper
2 teaspoons ground cumin
2 teaspoons Jerk seasoning
2 teaspoons lime Juice, fresh squeezed
5 ¼ cups vegetable or chicken stock

Combine ingredients in a saucepan on the stove. Bring to a boil. Transfer to fondue pot with its own heat source. Use your favorite meat dippers.

SHRIMP & CHEESE FONDUE
½ cup cooked baby shrimp
½ cup diced tomatoes with green chilies
1 cup beer light beer
1 teaspoon freshly ground pepper
2 ¾ cups (11 ounces) shredded Cheddar cheese
2 teaspoons finely chopped garlic
3 tablespoons all-purpose flour
Toss the cheese with the flour in a bowl. Place a metal bowl over a saucepan, or double boiler, filled with two inches of water. Bring the water to a boil over high heat. Reduce the heat to medium and pour the beer into the bowl. Stir in the tomatoes with the green chilies and garlic using a fork. Cook for 30 seconds, stirring constantly. Add half the cheese and cook until melted, stirring constantly. Add remaining cheese a small amount at a time, stirring constantly in a circular motion after each addition until the cheese is melted. Fold in the shrimp and pepper. Pour into a warm fondue pot and keep warm over low heat. Use dippers of choice.

SIMPLE MILK CHOCOLATE FONDUE (alcohol optional)
½ cup cream
1 pound milk chocolate
3 tablespoons Kirsch, Cointreau, or Brandy (optional)
Warm cream in saucepan over low heat. Stirring constantly, add the chocolate, broken into small pieces. Continue stirring until chocolate is melted and well blended. Add liquor or brandy, if desired. Transfer to dish with its own heat source. Ideal for fruit dippers.

SKINNY CHOCOLATE FONDUE
¼ cup granulated sugar
¼ cup unsweetened cocoa
1 cup water
1 teaspoon vanilla extract
2 teaspoons corn starch
Salt
Mix cornstarch and water in a small saucepan. When smooth, add remaining ingredients except fruit and stir over moderately high heat until mixture boils 1 minute. Pour into fondue pot to keep warm. Use dippers of your choice.

SPECTACULAR SPINACH FONDUE (large batch)

¼ cup onions, chopped
¼ teaspoon garlic oil or juice
¼ teaspoon salt
1 ¼ cup sour cream
1 lb. cream cheese
2 dashes of hot pepper sauce of your choice
3 ½ ounces of frozen spinach, chopped and drained well
4 ounces of water chestnuts, lightly chopped

At medium speed, blend cream cheese and sour cream thoroughly. Add remaining ingredients and blend.

Refrigerate 2-3 hours. Pour into fondue pot with its own heat source to keep mix warm. Serve with crusty French or Italian bread.

SPICY CRAB FONDUE (alcohol)

¼ cup white dry wine
¼ teaspoon garlic salt
½ teaspoon cayenne pepper
½ teaspoon Worcestershire sauce
1 cup crab meat, drained and flaked
1 package of cream cheese (8 oz. package)
5 ounces of sharp cheddar cheese
8 ½ ounce size
French bread, cut into cubes

Combine cheeses in small pot until melted and smooth. Add remaining ingredients. Stir well. If too thick, add additional wine. Pour into fondue pot with its own heat source to keep mix warm. Serve with breadsticks or bread chunks of your choice.

STRAWBERRY FIELDS FONDUE

1 cup vanilla yogurt
Grated rind from one orange
One can or tin of strawberries in juice

As you grate the rind of the orange, be careful to just get the orange rind, not the bitter white pith. Drain the strawberries from the tin, discarding the juice. Put the strawberries into the fondue pot and mash with the back of a fork. Add the yogurt and orange rind. Serve well-chilled, with cubes of plain sponge or plain biscuits to dip.

SUBLIME SWEETCORN FONDUE

1 lb. frozen sweetcorn kernels
1 ounce of butter
2 teaspoon corn flour
3 tablespoons of heavy cream
Few drops Tabasco sauce
Salt and pepper to taste

Put sweetcorn in a saucepan with 2 tablespoons water and simmer for a few minutes until tender. Drain and add to a blender. Process until mixture is just soft. In a saucepan, blend corn flour smoothly with cream. Add sweetcorn mixture and cook over a low heat until smooth. Pour mixture into fondue pot and season with salt, pepper and Tabasco sauce, then beat in butter. Use low heat source to keep warm. Serve with a selection of cooked shellfish.

TANGERINE DREAM FONDUE

1 can (14 ounces) fat-free sweetened condensed milk
6 ounces semisweet chocolate baking chips
8 tangerines, peeled and segmented

Cook milk and chocolate chips in heavy saucepan on very low heat, stirring constantly until chips melt (about 3 minutes). Transfer to fondue pot, and keep warm. Dip tangerine sections into sauce.

TERRIFIC TERIYAKI FONDUE (alcohol)

½ bunch spring onions shredded
½ cup soy sauce
1 small head Chinese leaves
1 small red pepper seeded and finely sliced
1 tablespoon wine vinegar
1 teaspoon ground ginger
2 cloves garlic crushed
2 lbs. fillet steak
3 teaspoons light soft brown sugar
6 tablespoon sunflower oil
6 tablespoons dry sherry
8 ounces fresh beansprouts

Cut steak into thin strips ½ inch wide and 4" long. Put 1 teaspoon of sugar and 2 tablespoons of soy sauce into a bowl and set aside. In a large bowl combine remaining sugar and soy sauce sherry garlic and ginger. Add strips of meat and leave to marinate for 1 hour. Weave the strips of meat onto fondue fork to cook until tender. <u>Create side salad:</u> Shred the Chinese leaves and place into a bowl with beansprouts, pepper and spring onions. Add oil to reserved sugar and soy sauce then whisk in vinegar and pour over salad. Toss lightly together. Add cooked meat.

TOMATO GARDEN FONDUE (alcohol)
½ pint tomato juice (half pint)
1 ½ tablespoon corn starch
1 ½ tablespoons butter
1 ½ tablespoons concentrated tomato pulp
2 dashes of sugar
2 tablespoons of Grappa or Kirsch
3 clove garlic, finely chopped
3/16 pint red wine
4 ounces cheese, grated
8-9 ounces Gruyere cheese
Salt and black pepper
Heat the butter in a fondue dish and sauté garlic. Add tomato juice, tomato pulp and sugar, bring to a boil.
Remove from heat and add cheese and stir. Return to heat and stir continuously until the cheese has melted. Blend the corn starch with the red wine, stir into cheese. Bring back to a boil and stir continuously. Season with salt and pepper, stir the grappa in the fondue. Pair with your favorite dipper and wine for sipping.

TOTALLY TOFFEE FONDUE
¼ cup milk
¼ cup strong black coffee
½ cup milk chocolate chips
1 large package of caramels
Place caramels, milk, coffee and chocolate chips in top of double boiler; cook over boiling water, stirring, until melted and blended. Pour into fondue pot with its own heat source to keep mix warm. Spear your choice of fruits, marshmallows and cake for dipping.

VEGETARIAN DELIGHT FONDUE

¼ cup milk
¼ cup white wine
1 (8 ounce) package shredded cheddar cheese
1 (8 ounce) package shredded Monterey Jack cheese
1 (8 ounce) package cream cheese, softened
¼ cup chopped green onions
¼ cup frozen chopped spinach, thawed and drained
1 teaspoon ground dry mustard
1 teaspoon ground cayenne pepper
1 teaspoon garlic powder
1 teaspoon coarsely ground black pepper

In a medium saucepan over medium heat, mix together milk, white wine, Cheddar cheese, Monterey Jack cheese and cream cheese. Cook, stirring frequently, until melted, about 10 minutes. Stir in green onions, spinach, dry mustard, cayenne pepper, garlic powder and black pepper. Continue cooking until all ingredients are well blended, about 10 minutes. Transfer mixture to a double boiler or fondue pot to keep warm. Perfect for roasted or raw veggie dippers.

VEGGIE VICTORY FONDUE

¼ cup butter, diced
½ medium swede
1 ¼ cups chicken stock (about 10 ounces)
1 small onion
1 small turnip
2 sticks celery
8 ounces carrots
Pinch of freshly grated nutmeg
Salt and black pepper to taste

Chop all vegetables finely, then put into a saucepan with stock. Bring to the boil and simmer until just tender. Drain vegetables and leave to cool slightly. Puree vegetables in a blender or food processor, then pass the puree through a strainer into the fondue pot. Place the pot over a low heat and gradually beat in the butter. Season with salt, pepper and nutmeg and keep hot over the burner. Goes great with sausages and/or potatoes.

VELVET ROPE FONDUE

1 tablespoon coffee liqueur
1/3 cup heavy whipping cream
4 ounces premium milk chocolate
For fun, add 4-6 drops red food coloring
Heat the cream in a small saucepan over low heat on your stovetop. Once simmering, stir in chocolate and liqueur. Stir the mixture continuously until all of the chocolate melts. Pour into fondue pot with its own heat source to keep mix warm. Serve this red velvet treat with fruit.

VERY BERRY FONDUE

½ cup caster sugar
1 lb. mixed summer fruits
6 teaspoons of corn flour
Pinch of mixed spice
Put the fruits into a saucepan with the sugar and 5 fl. ounces of water, and cook gently until tender. Crush fruits slightly with a potato masher and add the mixed spice. In a small bowl, blend the corn flour smoothly with a little water. Add this to the fruit in the pan and cook until thickened, stirring constantly. Bring to a boil. Transfer to fondue pot with its own heat source. Use dippers of your choice.

VERY VEGAN POTATO FONDUE (alcohol)

1 ½ teaspoon salt
1 cup dry white wine
1 pinch ground nutmeg
1 tablespoons olive oil
10 small boiling potatoes, peeled (1 lb.)
2 large onions, peeled and chopped
2 tablespoons cornstarch
2 tablespoons nutritional yeast
3 cloves garlic, minced
Cook potatoes in boiling, salted water 5 to 8 minutes, or until soft. Drain, and set aside. Heat oil in medium saucepan over medium-low heat. Add onions, and cook 15 to 20 minutes, or until soft and translucent. Add garlic, and cook 1 to 2 additional minutes. Meanwhile, dissolve cornstarch in 2 cups cold water in a small cup. Add cornstarch mix to onion mixture, increase heat to medium, and simmer for 5 minutes, stirring occasionally. Add yeast and salt, and simmer 5 minutes more, stirring occasionally. Remove from heat, add potatoes and ½ cup wine. Blend with traditional blender until smooth. Return to heat, and simmer gently 5 minutes. Add remaining ½ cup wine, and cook 1 minute,

stirring once or twice, or until fondue thickens. Transfer to fondue pot, sprinkle with nutmeg, and serve with dippers. Try green apples!

WHITE CREAM FONDUE (alcohol)
1 ounces cherry brandy
12 ounces white chocolate
8 ounces double cream
Combine the chocolate and cream in a bowl over a pan of hot water (or use a double boiler), and stir until the chocolate melts completely. Remove the bowl from the heat and stir in the cherry brandy. Put the mixture in a fondue pot to keep warm. Serve with pieces of fruit or firm cake.

WHITE WINE SWIRL FONDUE (alcohol)
¼ cup cherry brandy
½ clove garlic (optional)
1 lb. Swiss cheese, grated
2 cup dry white wine
2 dashes nutmeg
3 tablespoon flour
Black pepper
Rub pot walls with butter. Dredge cheese with flour. Heat wine on stove to about 150°. Add cheese by the handful, stirring until melted before each new addition. When all cheese has melted and mixture bubbles, add all seasonings...pepper, nutmeg and brandy. Keep it slow...simmering should take about 20 minutes. Keep heat on the low side to prevent burning. French bread, crisped in oven and broken into hunks is the ideal dipper for this one.

WORLD TRAVELER CHEESE FONDUE (alcohol)
1 cup of white wine
1 teaspoon roasted garlic, chopped
3 teaspoons shallots, diced
2 tablespoons dates, chopped
3- 3 ½ cups (try a 50-50 blend of Fontina and Gruyere cheese)
1 teaspoon of white truffle oil (try the specialty section at local supermarket)
Turn heat source to HIGH, place pot with 2" water on burner. Place liner into pot. When steam is visible, reduce heat to MED. Add white wine to the liner, while stirring with a fork; add garlic, shallots and dates to liquid. Stir for approx. 30-seconds making sure all chopped pieces are separated from each other. Add 1/3 of cheese and stir until fully incorporated into liquid. Add a second 1/3 of the cheese and continue stirring. Then add the rest of the cheese and stir using a circular whipping motion until smooth. You will know when you are done adding the cheese by the consistency of the fondue. Cheese age,

weather conditions, and time are all factors that may affect the amount of cheese that will go into your finished fondue. Add truffle oil and fold in with fork. Then remove fork from liner and enjoy.

Bonus
TURTLE FLAMBE FONDUE (alcohol)

½ - 1 cup caramel
1 ounce chopped pecans
1/3 ounce rum (may substitute with any flambé liquor)
2 large Symphony chocolate candy bars

Melt all ingredients into a double boiler fondue pot, heat mixture of chocolate and caramel to about 135 degrees. Stir frequently (to thin, just add a little milk). Slowly pour liquor into fondue pot. Ignite by touching a lighted match to the side of the pot. After flame burns, sprinkle nuts over chocolate. This recipe is amazing with brownie bites, fruit, and pretzels.

DIABETIC CHOCOLATE FONDUE

1 cup skim milk
1 teaspoon vanilla or ½ to ¾ teaspoon rum extract
One (8-ounce) package unsweetened baking chocolate
Artificial sweetener such as Equal or Splenda (14½ teaspoons of the baking variety or 48 individual packets or 2 cups of the spoonful variety)

Chop small bits of chocolate and heat with milk in medium saucepan over medium-low to low heat, whisking constantly, until chocolate is almost melted. Remove from heat; continue whisking until chocolate is fully melted and mixture is shiny. Add artificial sweetener and vanilla or rum extract, whisking until mixture is smooth. Pour chocolate mixture into fondue pot with its own heat source to keep warm. Serve with a selection of fresh fruit pieces and pretzels for dipping.

Thank you for your purchase!
May you enjoy and be well!

ABOUT THE AUTHOR

I am a Tennessee native and a connoisseur of great tastes. My culinary delights are inspired by my Southern roots.

I am from cornbread and cabbage, fried chicken and Kool-Aid soaked lemon slices.

I am from hen houses, persimmon trees and juicy, red tomatoes on the vine.

I am from sunflowers growing wild in summer and homemade ice cream in the winter.

I am from family reunions, blue collar men, happy housewives, and Sunday dinners.

I am from spiritual folks who didn't always get it right, but believed in the power of prayer – and taught it to their kids.

I am from the hottest of hot summers and kids running barefoot and free through thirsty Tennessee grass.

I am from a grandmother who sang gospel that was magic…song drenched air would tumble from her lungs, leap into your spirit and make you feel fantastic things.

I am from hard, heartfelt lessons about living and kitchens full of the perfume of love.

♥♥♥ This book is from my heart to yours. ♥♥♥

Find more cookbooks online at http://www.tinyurl.com/sodelishdish.
For freebies & new book announcements, follow @SoDelishDish on social media!

Scan with your smartphone!

Made in the USA
Middletown, DE
17 December 2017